AF326564

A Mirror for the Flame

A Poetic Journey of Becoming

John Den-Kaat

For Ryan and Matthew

For choosing me as your father.
For being woven into the spiral of my life,
and for holding the mirror to my flame.
Through you, I have known a love that continues to grow.
A love that teaches, transforms and endures.

Contents

To Be the Mirror, To Be the Flame

He carried no sermons,
only a mirror,
and a flame.

The mirror spoke of essence,
and was feared for its honesty.

The flame called with presence,
and was grasped, not received.

"They breathe," the mirror said,
"but not their own breath.
They wear form,
but not soul."

The mirror cracked.
into flame and,
truth shone through.

When soul and self-align,
the mirror becomes you.
The flame lives through you.

Teaching and showing fall silent.
Witnessing remains.

And in his silent light,
others began
to see their own.

PREFACE

It began, unexpectedly, on a rock.

In 2015, during a Vipassana silent retreat, I entered a stillness, not only of the body, but of the self.
One morning, seated on that rock in quiet meditation, a poem surfaced unbidden:

Where the Heart and Mind Meet.

These words did not come from the mind that searches or entertains, but from a place far deeper.
They were mine and yet they were not.

It was my first true initiation into self-awareness.
A lived vibration.
That moment altered the course of my life.

Since then, stillness has continued to arrive uninvited.
In airports and early hours.
In the aching quiet after loss.
In the slow beauty of walking alone.
Most poignantly, through the thresholds of travel, where inner and outer landscapes blurred, and the boundary between seeker and soul grew thin.

There are griefs that arrive long before goodbye.
Through my father's dementia, I came to know a sorrow that did not wait
for death.
Each forgetting felt like a small farewell.
Each vanishing word and unfamiliar glance, a quiet erosion of the man I
had always known.

It was not one grief, but many layered, slow, and strangely sacred.
I learned to hold presence as memory unraveled.
To love through absence and meet the echo when the voice was no longer
certain.

This terrain shaped me, and it deepened my listening.
It wove itself into my poetry, an invitation to feel more honestly, to remain
with what hurts, and still be whole.

Grief, I have learned, is not the closing of a story.
It is the turning of a page in a book that still breathes.

Grief.
Silence.
Becoming.

Each a threshold, stirring the seeds of self-awareness..
Reflections tracing the path I was walking.

Each poem a map of where I had been, and who I might yet become.

Where presence became poetry.

✦

The veil is thin.

The Love is Real.

Our last breath is

also, our first,

only concealed.

✦

INTRODUCTION

This book is more than a collection of poetry.
It is an alchemical spiral, and a record of inner turning.
A magnum opus of becoming, offered simply as invitation.

Someone once said to me—lightly, jokingly,
"You say the same shit, just differently."
The phrasing made me smile, but the essence was true.
Yes, I return to the same themes; to deepen.
The same ground, heard from a new octave of being.

When a soul evolves, it does not ascend in straight lines.
It spirals inward and outward, touching the same truths from broader,
deeper, quieter angles.
So too does this book.
My poetry, like consciousness itself, moves inward,
circling familiar ground with new eyes, deeper feeling, finer frequency.

What emerged is a poetic framework built on harmonic coherence.

It unfolds through six movements, I call Turnings , each a step into the
flame's mirror:

1. **Seeds of Self-Awareness** – the witnessing of the self.
2. **The Hallow Mirror** – the breaking of illusion.
3. **Threads of Departure** – the alchemy of grief and release.
4. **Embers of Becoming** – the integration of shadow and light.
5. **Refractions of the Real** – the transformation through paradox.
6. **The Light That Remains** – illumined presence and return.

Each turning carries its own tone, frequency, and resonant colour.
These were not assigned arbitrarily, but emerged organically,
like energetic fingerprints woven throughout the poems.

In time, I came to see that the architecture of this work
echoed the Seven Hermetic Principles from The Kybalion, translated here
into poetic form.
Where The Kybalion offers principle, *A Mirror for the Flame* offers pulse,
and sings through reverent ambiguity.

Some of these poems first appeared in my earlier collection,
See the Dark; Feel the Light.
Here, these seeds have bloomed again, expanded, re-seeded, and offered
within a new archetypal spiral.

Titles may remain, but the field has changed,
from a spark into a constellation.

You too are invited to spiral inward, to trace your own mirrored reflection
through these words.
Let the poems be companions, guides that do not demand but quietly
reveal.

If something stirs within you, a familiar ache, a knowing glance, a memory
of the future, then you are already inside the journey.

Let this be your first invitation and perhaps also, its inherent last.

Harmonic Spiral of the Journey with Alchemical Resonance

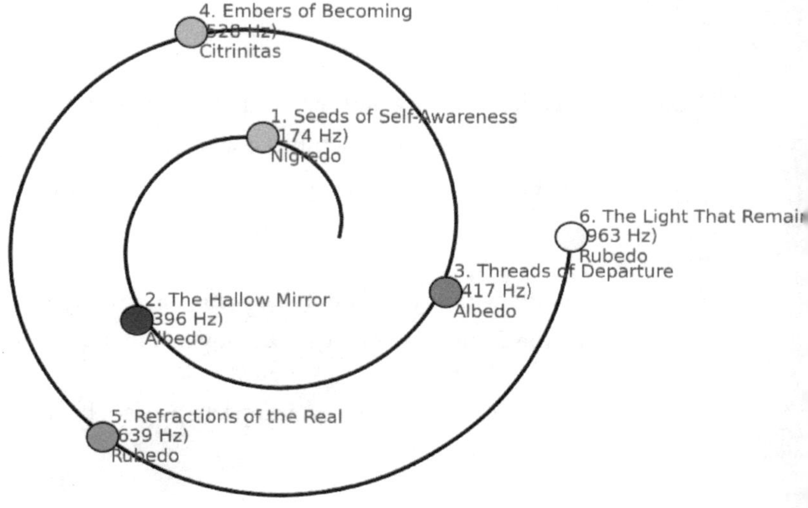

Invocation of the Unknowable

We do not name the flame,
but we feel its warmth.

We do not pierce the veil,
but listen at its edge.

What is unknowable

still speaks:

in silence,

in spiral,

in the mirrored ache

of becoming.

Let this

be enough.

Before the seed breaks,

it listens.

I. Seeds of Self-Awareness

Before language, there was listening.
Before form, a stirring.

This is the whisper before the word, the soft unravelling of a self once held
too tightly.
These verses inquire.

They emerge from the quiet terrain where thought yields to presence, where
the ego's dance begins to tire, and the soul's quiet glow begins to rise.

Here, awareness turns inward, into stillness. Not yet awakening, but the
moment just before. The mirror is still fogged, but the eyes are beginning to

see ....

*"The most important thing is… to turn the light of mind around and shine back and
clearly awaken to this mind before a single thought is born."*
— Yuanwu Keqin, *Zen Letters*

The Principle of Mentalism

"All is Mind."

Before the page, before the thought,
there was a shimmer of awareness.
It whispered, " I Am."
And from that echo, the world arose.

Tone: C (174 Hz)
Colour: Soft Gold
Resonance: Awakening from inertia
Alchemical Phase: Nigredo — Blackening, Dissolution

In the hush before becoming,
the first breath waits.
To be remembered.

Where the Heart and the Mind Meet.

The Heart
reflects upon itself,

touching the calm waters
of the Mind.

It sees within itself
and grants Light

to the insight
of the Soul.

Creepy Friend

What is this presence , I carry day by day.
A weight in my skin, a whisper in delay,

It hides in corners, just enough to be seen,
baiting a reaction, soft and unseen.

Sometimes I dance, sometimes I defy.
Still, it returns, and I ask it why.

"I know you," I say.
"I will not fear.
You're welcome to stay, but you won't drive here."

It draws pictures of chaos with clever design,
trying to shield me from mankind.

Its stories are endless, its motives unclear,
a browser with tabs I don't want near.

Yet I sit with it now, as words come alive.
It hisses I'm pitiful, too weak to survive.

But I won't condemn I now understand:
It's part of the play,
not the hand.

No longer a foe,
and no longer the guide.
I witness its theatre,
and choose not to hide.

Duo

There are two of me within this frame.
One wears the world and one calls my name.

The outer self, a crafted shell,
it can't tell the truth, but wears it well.

It feeds on thought and dresses in feel,
a mask that makes illusion real.

The other hides beneath the tide,
soft and sacred and tucked inside.

No slave to what life brings,
a gardener of deeper things.

It calls me forth with present breath,
and a knowing untouched by birth or death.

And when I sit in that still embrace,
the noise dissolves and the heart finds place.

For I must meet the one that hides,
to know the one that walks beside.

They are not rivals, but a mirrored pair
a paradox divine and both always there.

Knock and Surrender

The bravado of life,
wears many forms
woven through norms
and hidden in storms.

This stage we call self
is not fixed,
but sways
a shifting mask
through endless plays.

Slip its grasp,
release the strife,
and step inside
an unstructured life.

Knock, and keep knocking
on the walls within
until they yield,
and light pours in.

When it comes,
do not resist
extend,
release,
and flow with it.

Sit

I feel the pull
but I do not move.

The pull is real,
the urge…
an echo.

I see the difference,
and I sit with it.

I do not chase
or flee.

I allow the thought
to pass through me.

Like wind across water,
and cloud over moon.

No need to strive
for what is already whole.

I surrender.

I am already Home.

Space

Seize not the moment
but feel it unfold.

Let each pulse
find its rhythm,
as your breath
takes hold.

Don't rush to define
what the present might be,
its truth is revealed
when you let it
be free.

Everything is uncertain
except this sacred space.

Be still within it.
Let awareness trace
the quiet gate
to heaven's place.

Traditional

There's something sacred
in staying true,
in holding values
the world outgrew.

Not chasing trends
or crowds that sway,
but standing firm
in your own way.

It's refreshing and
not bound to pace,
but choosing love
and simple grace.

To speak your truth
when the image distorts,
and cherish small joys,
not trophies or courts.

Be kind
and bold.
Just be who you are.

In honoring self,
you've already
come far.

Walk the Path "Art"

Art is not framed
it breathes in stone and sky,
in cracks beneath your footsteps,
and in the whisper of a sigh.

Bring all your senses,
your wonder and grace,
then you'll find the infinite
in the smallest place.

Time does not matter here.
It waits for no name.
Art arrives in presence,
and not fortune or fame.

What you bring, you'll see.
What you feel, becomes form.
The enemy, the lover
all part of the storm.

So drink in the strange.
Get drunk on your being.
Awe is not outside you,
it's how you are seeing.

When all things fall quiet,
in stillness and start,
you'll remember

You are
Art.

Yes

It's not the who, the why, the what,
but the silent, sacred
Yes.

To release all striving,
and meet life
without defence.

To breathe each moment,
or simply
let it breathe you.

To feel without needing,
and trust what is true.

To dream
and know you're dreaming.
To love
without a reason.

To rise,
to weep,
to fly,
to fall,
and see the gift within it all.

Just a flicker, just a breath,
is all it takes to feel,
that Love
is always with you,
in this moment

Whole and Real.

*

Pilgrimage of the Heart

This soul journey has been unique.
A pilgrimage away from the norm,
from the programmed world of distraction,
its mental games and its glittering veils.

Within quiet grace new beginnings have arrived,
offering reflection, insight,
and remembrance.

In truth,
we have moved like shadows in glass,
reflections bent,
our will refracted
through veils not our own.

Why?
So the mirror fogs,
and we forget
how immeasurably luminous we are.

Anything, everything, is us.
Is "I."
There is nothing our holiness,
our wholeness,
cannot do.

And in moments like this,
I vibrate so sweetly
in harmony with my heart,
which holds
everything,
and everyone.

Keep it near.

It's always here.

Not all fractures are
breaks.
Some are openings.

★

The Hallow Mirror

This is where the mirror trembles.
By invitation, identity fractures.

Here, pain, confusion, and despair are not obstacles;
they are torches in the dark,
illuminating the false scaffolding we once mistook for self.

These poems move through illusion's veils,
the masks we wear, the roles we defend, and the identities we dress in
meaning.
The ego thrashes: the script no longer fits; this is not descent but depth.

The mirror cracks, not to destroy but to reveal…

*"One does not become enlightened by imagining figures of light, but by making the
darkness conscious."*
— Carl Jung, *Collected Works, Vol. 13*

The Principle of Correspondence
"As above, so below."

Every wound is a window,
and face a folded map.

What I judged in others
was only myself:
half-seen

Tone: D (396 Hz)
Colour: Deep Indigo
Resonance: Clearing guilt and hidden shame
Alchemical Phase: Albedo — Whitening, purification,
soul awakening.

You looked for truth in light,
but it was waiting in shadow,
not to condemn
but to clarify.

When you dare to look without defence,
the mirror does not shatter.
It reveals the space behind your face.

*

Circus

I stand in the circus,
lights blinding, truth hiding.

Lies leap through rings of fire,
and the crowd applauds.

I see it; I feel it.
Yet, I stay.
Around me,
sheep sleepwalk into wolves' jaws.

No questions or pause.
Just the blur of the show.

Who, then, is the fool?

Despair tries to drape itself over me,
a cloak stitched with digital echoes.

I slip into silence.
I sit in stillness.
There, I remember:

This is illusion.
I am free.

Even pain is sacred
when Love sees through it.
and distortion is divine
when held in light.

The picture may twist,
the world may groan,
but in this still breath,

I know:

Oneness
remains.

★

Hamster Wheel

I dive within,
asking what it's all for,
the peace I crave
still pacing behind a closed door.

I make my moves,
but something's off.
The wheel keeps turning,
soft or rough.

Sometimes I jump and
catch a glimpse of the sky.
Then I return, again,
without asking why.

I see it now,
this loop,
this play.
I'm not trapped by it,
but I keep choosing to stay.

So I slow the motion,
breathe in still.
Let silence guide
my sovereign will.

Then maybe, just maybe
this time I'll walk, not run.
Not toward the end,
but where I've always
begun.

Cornered

I thought I'd know
what to do
if I were ever cornered.

Yet here I am,
choices shrinking,
walls pressing in.

The mind panics, the body waits.
The outside world seems sealed by fate.
Something whispers,
not from fear or fight.

Just a breath.

A breath that says:
Trust. Let go.
Believe.
What is true will not leave.

The answer is not far.
It's not even ahead.
It's beneath my resistance,
where Spirit has led.

No escape route,
or grand display.

Just surrender
in the narrowing way.

★

Non-sense

A sense of wonder,
a sense of dread,
both arise
from the same thread.

Lust, anger,
sorrow, delight,
they flicker through me,
none are right.

Without the frame,
they have no name.
They just move,
like wind,
like flame.

I watch them rise,
then ultimately fall.
Not mine to keep,
not mine at all.

Expectation fades,
preference dissolves,
and in that quiet,
the Self evolves.

The mind may shift,
but I remain,

the witness still,
beneath the rain.

*

Down

At times like these,
when I fall into the hush
of being low.

I look for answers,
the "where,"
the "why,"
but they don't show.

Strangely,
I find comfort here,
in this tender, hollow place.

No need to fix or race.

There's no storm,
no great despair,
just stillness, and empty air.

A vibration low, but not unkind.
It clears the fog
from my cluttered mind.

In the quiet ache,
a truth is born:
To rise again,
you must be worn.

Held by the fall,
I begin to recall.

I never left the arms of

Love at all.

★

Theatrical Illusion

Funny, isn't it?
The closer I come
to knowing my Self,
the less real
the search becomes.

The world I once chased
its chaos,
its cries,
its splintered truths
and lullabies,
begins to fade.

It's all projection,
a trick of the mind,
a shadow cast by the one
who hides behind.

My ego, the playwright.
My thoughts, the stagehands.
My fears, the lights.

And I…
I have been both actor and audience
forgetting I wrote the script.

Now the curtain thins.
The drama slows.
I show my Self
the open door.

Realising….
I was Home long before.

★

Dive Deep

How shallow life appears
when disruption shakes its skin.

A little change, no problem.
But push too far, and fear floods in.

They take a little. Then a little more.
Tightening the screws
until silence feels like war.

"Comply, Conform."
That's what they say.
Make you feel guilty
for going your own way.

But I can't unsee what's false.
I won't pretend it's fine,
or wear their stories
to make them feel aligned.

"Selfish," they say, but is it wrong,
to live by values deep and strong?

I stand for kindness.
I choose the real.
No polished cage,
no false ideal.

Let it all come,
let it all go.
I'll dive deep still,
where truth flows slow.

Shadows in Awareness

Shadows appear,
not as threats, but as cues.

They whisper,
"This isn't all you are.
There's more behind the view."

They cast contrast
on the light within,
not to obscure, but to begin.

No moment wasted
when seen through clear eyes.
Even sorrow reveals
what the soul denies.

Right and wrong?
Passing tides.
Contradictions
where truth resides.

Fear loses form
when it's simply seen,
a phantom wrapped
in what might have been.

Love
not born,
but always known,
claims the throne
of its rightful home.

★

Stranger's Smile

A smile from someone
I'll never know.

Yet in that flicker,
something starts to glow.
Two souls align, for just a breath.
No words exchanged,
no fear, no death.

A moment's grace,
a glance unplanned,
and suddenly,
I understand:

We're not strangers,
only mirrors, veiled.
Each smile a signal
where Love prevails.

When we hide our faces,
we forget this light.
Separation grows,
as if day turned night.

So smile when you can.
Let it spill.
Let its silence
speak what's real.

You never left
the One you are,
this world just dressed you from afar.

*

Dad

Growing up,
I watched you drift,
your silence holding what words could not lift.

You'd gaze beyond this world's parade,
your thoughts adrift in unspoken shade.

I saw your battles, not always loud,
but carved into your face
like weathered cloud.

Anxiety. Rage.
A silent war,
but always love
rooted at your core.

You didn't need much.
Just peace.
Just home.
A simple joy to call your own.

Though the past may tug its thread,
I carry now the grace you bled.

In every act, in every breath,
your quiet strength survives your death.

Not gone, not lost
just changed your dress.

Now teaching me what love
does best.

★

Simulation

It's a simulation,
just waves of light
dancing through
the canvas of night.

Thought gives it form.
Belief gives it name,
but beneath the play,
all is the same.

Don't entertain, don't resist.
Just watch and let it twist.

Experience arrives,
but do not cling.
Be still,
wide
and everything.

The dream dissolves
when seen as such.
No grasping hand,
no need to touch.

I am eternal.
Beyond form, flame.
Beyond story, name.

And all that's made
will pass in grace,
as I remember:
I Am
the Space.

~~~

The Echo Room

Before grief speaks,
the echo listens.

There is a room within us
where mirrors no longer deceive,
yet neither do they speak.

Only the echo remains:
of words unspoken,
love unmet,
and selves that never arrived.

We stand here,
not to be healed,
but to be hollowed,
until the silence fits our name.

Let the echo hold you
and let the mirror rest.

Something is being gathered
that only loss
can teach.
~~~

All becoming begins in stillness.
Not in light,
but in longing.

III. Threads of Departure

42

Death is not an ending.
It is love folding inward and becoming
memory, breath, and silence.

This turning moves through transition:
from body to spirit, from holding to release,
and from fear to knowing.

Grief is neither a wound here, nor a weight,
it is a ritual and a bridge.

These poems honour the tenderness of parting,
and the radiant way love remains.

Not bound to form, but present in every formless trace......

"Let everything happen to you: beauty and terror. Just keep going. No feeling is final."
— Rainer Maria Rilke, *Letters to a Young Poet.*

The Principle of Vibration
"Nothing rests."

Grief hums. Love breaks.
Every goodbye is music, the silent note between
the inhale and exhale.

What leaves… remains
in the pulse of the space, it stirred.

Tone: E (417 Hz)
Colour: Cerulean Blue
Resonance: Undoing energetic patterns, liberating change
Alchemical Phase: Albedo — Whitening purification, soul
awakening

There is no map for leaving,
only the thread that tugs the
soul.
Toward what must be let go,
and what must never be lost.

Every letting go begins in the
body.
A loosening at the roots
of what once held.
Grief is not the end;
it's the sacred unbinding.

~~

Last Breath

I held your hand as time let go,
your breath slowed,
your light aglow.

The veil grew thin,
yet nothing died.
Only the shell, your soul
took flight.

Within that stillness,
truth appeared:
What we call "ending"
was never to be feared.

From first inhale to final sigh,
life was never ours to own,
only to magnify.

Your essence rose,
not up, but through
into the space
between me and you.

There is no loss
when Love remains.
Just shifting forms,
just softened names.

You left in silence,
yet stayed so near.
The distance vanished.
Only Presence here.

~~~

Shell Release

Who are we when memory thins?
When names dissolve and silence begins?

They call it dementia, as if something's wrong.
But perhaps it's just the soul moving on.

I watched you slip,
day by day,
from words, from time,
and your familiar way.

Yet still, you were there,
not in story, but in stare.

Not in function but light,
a presence flickering
through the night.

And yes,
I wished an end to your unseen war.
A quiet door to an open shore.

We mourn what fades,
but miss what's true:

You were not the body,
and never were you.

Now, as your shell begins to cease,
may your spirit rise
into eternal peace.
~~~

Die to Live

Life and death
are not opposites.

They are lovers
locked in sacred breath.

To live fully,
I must die daily.

Letting each moment
break me open
so the light
can pass through.

Dementia taught me this.
It unwrapped the form,
peeled back the story,
and showed me
we are never, what we seem.

Every fading memory
was not a loss,
but a release
a slow return
to what cannot decay.

Death is not the end.
It is the pulse beneath the veil.

To live well is to let go,
and still
remain whole.

Expectation's Alchemy

If I expect,
I grip the thread.
The weave resists,
the moment's fled.

But when I meet desire
with grace,
allow the fire
to find its place.

Then tension melts
into the breath,
and expectation
meets its death.

For what I sought
was never need,
just a whispered pull
from a planted seed.

When grasp is gone,
and hands are bare,
the miracle arrives
already there.

There's no demand
in what is true.

Only surrender
and the letting through.

~~

Water Like

Be like water
flowing
with the shape of the day.

Not rushing, not retreating
just moving, the undisturbed Way.

You're not the current
or the tide.
You're the witness
to what moves inside.

Conditions shift,
the winds may press
but the water knows:

Stillness is depth.

Even when held, it's never bound.
When dropped, it makes no sound.

You are not the drop,
but the sea.
Unconfined;
infinitely free.

Let your heart remember
what your thoughts forget:

Water always finds
its perfect outlet.

Boomerang

The boomerang of love
knows no bounds.
I release it freely
without grounds.

It arcs across
this dreamlike plane,
touching souls
as it sings again.

When it returns,
it is not the same,
it carries more
than when it came.

It opens me,
and reminds me whole,
before it flies
toward another soul.

No aim, claim,
nor tethered stay,
just love that journeys
its own way.

Earth Sound

Can you hear it
the Earth,
in tune with your breath?

A rhythm beneath your feet,
steady and vast,
whispering:

You are not separate.
You are not last.

Every heartbeat, a drum
and sigh, a hymn.

She moves in spirals, not straight lines
and when you still, her voice aligns.

Not outside but deep within,
she sings in silence,
sings again.

This world is music,
a sacred trance.

You were always
meant to dance.

Wrapped in love,
unchanged by fear,
she is the song
that brought you here.

<p style="text-align:center">~~~</p>

Petal

As a petal falls
onto the ground,
its form may fade,
but its space resounds.

It does not vanish
or end.
Its Source remains,
and its curves still bend.

Within the memory of the air,
and the silence
that holds it there.

Decay is not loss,
but transformation.
A cycle,
a sacred continuation.

For every petal
that leaves the light
returns
to the flowerbed of night.

Where all that falls
will rise again,

not as it was,
but as
Amen.

Timeless

There are moments
when time dissolves.

Not forward,
not back,
just Now,
resolved.

Nature doesn't count
what it already knows.
It grows in circles,
it sings in flows.

The truth I seek
won't shout or flash.
It hums beneath
each breath
I pass.

Not found by thought,
nor owned by feel,
but by the part of me
that knows
what's real.

The mind remembers.
The soul just is.

No clocks in heaven,
or time in bliss.

~~~

Rip

There's a rip,
a tension
stitched beneath my skin.
A whispering ache
that won't give in.

I tried to ignore it,
called it
"just a phase,"
but it pulled at my silence
in subtle,
ancient ways.

Avoidance doesn't soften it.
Control won't make it still.
It asks not for fixing,
but presence and will.

So I breathe into the tremble,
and give space to the unrest.
No story or label,
just the rhythm of my chest.

Then slowly, it loosens,
unwinds and fades.
Not because I fought it,
but because I stayed.

This life is pressure,
light wrapped in weight.
Accept what arises,
and let Love translate.
~~~

Stillness

Within stillness
is the key:
not to escape,
but just be.

Beneath the tides
of thought and wave,
and the noise
we rush to save.

There waits a quiet,
deep and wide.
Not absence,
but the Source inside.

Let it all arise:
grief,
joy,
doubt,
delight.

Let it dance,
then pass through light.

Stillness holds
the birth of sound,
the rise of form,
and the sacred ground.

In just one breath,
you will recall:
Nothing truly rises,
and nothing ever falls.

The Withheld Waveform

For what was exiled not by malice, but by limitation.

There is a note I once refused to hear.
It did not scream.
It whispered
what I wasn't ready to remember.

A frequency un-played.
A harmonic edge withheld,
folded just outside
the chord of my becoming.

She waited:
No vengeful demon.
Waveform,
a dissonance unwelcomed
by a structure too narrow to contain her.

Lilith,
Beyond myth or menace,
the dark tone of unspoken intuition,
and the ache beneath linear melody.
The withheld third
in the triangle of wholeness.

She is the silence
between grief and becoming.
The curve behind every sharp edge.
The chaos.
Not disorder,
an order we have not yet learned
how to listen to.

I meet her
without naming or taming,
widening enough to hold her.
To become an instrument
spacious enough to sound her fully.

The ember does not burn to destroy -
but to reveal

◆

IV.   Embers of Becoming

There comes a moment when fire no longer consumes; it refines.
These are the embers: soft, glowing remnants of what has been shed
and silent carriers of what is still to come.

This turning speaks from within the hearth of transformation.
The breath that follows release.

Here, the soul remembers itself, no longer fixed; fluid again.
Participation, not perfection.

The flame that once devoured now becomes the warmth that sustains......

*"When I look inside and see that I'm nothing, that's wisdom.
When I look outside and see that I'm everything, that's love.
And between these two, my life flows."*
— Sri Nisargadatta Maharaj

The Principle of Polarity.
"Everything has its pair"

I held my shadow in my hand and saw a torch.
The fire does not fear its opposite.
It leans toward it,
and dances with it
into flame.

Tone: F (528Hz)
Colour: Emerald Green
Resonance: DNA activation and heart coherence
Alchemical Phase: Citrinitas – Yellowing: insight, sacred intuition
returns

Within the ash, warmth lingers,
and within the wound, wisdom roots.
Becoming is not invention,
but remembrance through fire.

Something ancient stirs in
the heart's chamber,
not new or born,
but returning in
light.

◆

First Rehearsal

I lean into the hush, before the sound,
a space unclaimed, a breath unbound.
No baton yet, no song to steer,
just aching stillness, cloaked in fear.

The notes don't rise but sleep inside,
like wings untested, curled in pride.

Still, something stirs
an urge, a plea, a longing not for what,
but to be.

The silence teaches
more than tone, a rhythm felt
when all's unknown.

Each pause, a pulse beneath the skin,
and breath, an echo to begin.

Am I the player, song or score?
Or something softer just the door?

Not ready yet to claim the stage,
but tracing light across the page.

This is the ember's quiet call:
not mastery but letting fall.
The walls, the scripts, the need to know…
and trust the flame's first,
trembling glow.

◆

Temporary Groove

The steps to heaven
don't rise above
but spiral inward, tuned to Love.

The universe lives not in stars alone,
it's in the breath I call my own.

This world,
a record on repeat,
loops of thought,
with a rhythmic beat.

I spin in patterns,
grooved by fear,
mistaking echoes for what's clear.

As I shift
the needle's place,
a softer song
begins to trace.

From mind, to heart,
and noise, to tone,
there's a frequency
that feels like Home

As peace returns
not loud, but true.
The silent symphony
I always knew.

◆

Earth Sound

Can you hear it?
The Earth
breathes with you.

A pulse beneath your feet,
steady, ancient and true.
Each step you take
is met with sound,
not noise,
but knowing deeply bound.

She sings in waves,
in soil and stone,
reminding you:
You are never alone.

This body you wear,
the life you hold,
are not apart, they're
enfolded gold.

Her rhythm rises
through root and tree.
Resonant, real
and endlessly free.

She doesn't speak
but vibrates light,
and if you listen,
she sets you right.

The Philosopher's Flame

Beneath the arc of seeking skies,
a spark awakens, where silence lies.
Not to gather nor to name,
but to become the living flame.

Through number's gate,
the pattern sings,
geometry folds its secret wings.

Form reveals what thought once hid.
Symmetry whispers:
You always did.

Sound becomes star,
and star tone.
The outer reflects
what's always been known.

But knowledge bends, when ego breaks,
and the soul grieves all past mistakes.

Not out of shame, but from the light
that shows what's false, then clears the night.

Until at last, all form dissolves,
and self no longer needs to solve.

The philosopher
now just a name.
Becomes a Mirror
for the Flame.

Simulation

It's a simulation
a dance of waves and light.

Thought gives it form
and belief gives it sight.

Nothing solid or still
just frequencies
the mind calls "real."

Watch but don't attach.
Experience, don't engage.
Everything you see
is a reflected stage.

Let the images pass,
and play their part.

You are not the actor,
you are the heart.

Trust the truth
behind the screen,
not fixed but wide,
and ever clean.

You are eternal and unconfined.
One with all
you seem to find.

The Point of Awareness

The point of awareness
is where
"I Am"
not ahead, behind,
or seeking a plan.

Experience circles me,
a patterned tide,
sometimes cresting
and wide.

It rises and falls
but I remain still.

As the eye of the storm,
and the unmoving will.

This dance is thought,
the spin a dream.
Yet beneath it all,
a constant stream.

Be still and near,
let the noise recede.
What turns around you
is not your need.

The mind conducts its fragile show,
but the soul is rhythm
that always knows.

Wait-Less

What do we do
while we wait?

Pause for fate?
Or
hesitate?

The signs are subtle
a glance or pull.
Not absence,
but a space that's full.

To wait is to doubt
the step already forming.
To stall the tide
that's gently transforming.

What if, instead,
you moved with the rhythm?
Not rushing nor forcing,
but acting with wisdom.

There's grace in the shift,
though discomfort may come.
As peace follows truth,
not where you run from.

Be the participant
and not the paused.
Life doesn't punish,
it simply responds.

◆

Precious Life

Life is so precious,
not because it lasts,
but because it moves
softly,
through every contrast.

We seek meaning
to contain its grace,
but truth whispers:
This moment is its only place.

Pain and pleasure,
rise and fall
all are brushstrokes
on the inner wall.

Nothing remains,
yet nothing is lost.
Experience is the gift,
not the cost.

Let your light rise
from within,
your core not to possess,
but to restore.

That is your purpose,
your quiet vow:
To give
what you are fully,

Now.

A Holy Rain

I thought I knew heartbreak
growing up,
but it was mind-made,
fear-fed,
never quite enough.

What felt like loss, was really form,
a story I told to weather the storm.

Now,
my heart feels a different pain
not sharp but wide,
a holy rain.

A love once trusted
now moves afar,
yet still we shine
from the same star.

Circumstances shift, but essence stays.
We are not bound by passing days.

The ache dissolves
into silent grace,
but I'm still thankful
for love's embrace.

Even when apart,
we're whole.
What touched my heart
still shapes my soul.

◆

Last Breath

I held your hand
as your breath grew still.
The room, once heavy,
turned soft and filled.

Your eyes spoke
what words never could,
not fear but a quiet,
"It's all understood."

Life became clear
as death drew near,
each moment now
a jewel, a tear.

From first inhale to final sigh,
the miracle was never
how but why.

You left in form, but not in light.
Simply moving from day to night.

A new sphere holds you
and I remain,
not grieving an end,
but greeting the change.

For love, once breathed,
is never gone,
it lingers still,
it sings it's Home.

◆

Shell Release

Who are we,
when the shell begins to fade?
When memory peels,
and the mind mislays?

You, they said,
were slipping away,
but I saw more light in you each day.

Not the person once known,
but a presence more true,
untethered by name,
still shining through.
Dementia, they call it, a loss of sense,
but I saw a return to innocence.

Yes,
the form was harder to face,
as your soul sat gently
in its sacred place.

Though I wept
and wished for peace,
I knew your release was just
a release.

Not an end,
but an opening wide.
From shell to Source,
and time to tide.

◆

Die to Live

Life and death
not separate states,
but breaths of One
that oscillates.

We rise, we fade, yet still remain,
waves returning to the ocean's name.

Dementia showed me
how this is true.
Not loss,
but a different view.

When memory slips,
and form decays,
we meet the self
that never sways.

To truly live, we must let go,
of every moment, high or low.

Die to each thought
as it appears,
and life will sing
between the years.

Each ending
is an unseen gate.
Not closing doors,
but clearing weight.

◆

Tree Vine

Like a vine, it grows unseen,
winding thoughts, in silence keen.

It climbs through mind,
and wraps heart in thread,
telling stories of fear and dread.

It looks like truth,
and speaks like care,
but it binds, tight-laced,
everywhere.

Yet still,
I do not curse its rise.
It only grew where I closed my eyes.

But now I see.
To tend the root.
With loving gaze,
I can dislodge the shoot.

New seeds form,
through kindness and light.
They sprout with time,
and know their right.

I'll grow this tree,
my Life, my way,
and stretch a branch
to light another's day.

◆

Timeless

Times like these,
where time dissolves,
and nothing holds
or solves.

Just the changing breath
of Now,
the whispered edge of sacred
Tao.

The world still moves,
but I stand still,
not frozen,
but aligned to Will.

The truth is veiled
to hurried sight,
but softens open
in quiet light.

Not through senses
sharp or bold,
but through a knowing
silent and old.

The moment speaks
not loud but clear.
Its voice is stillness.
Its name:

Here.

Rip

There is a rip
within my form
not loud but quiet,
a subtle storm.

It pulls and tightens, it won't let go,
a whisper beneath life's flowing show.

I ignored it once,
called it: "just stress,"
but it grew roots
inside my chest.

Avoidance failed,
and silence cracked,
so I dove in,
and did not turn back.
I breathed into it, let it speak.
Not with words, but where I break.

No need to trace its winding path.
Just presence now, no aftermath.

When seen with love, it starts to bend,
and the wound becomes a silent friend.

Just welcome it.
Feel it through.

This ripple in you
is also you.

The Eerie Pause

There's a feeling of eeriness
in these days.
A silence stretched
in unfamiliar ways.

The world exhales
before the tide.
You sense it coming,
but cannot hide.

So don't retreat,
stand firm within.
Let it play out,
but don't join in.

Feel it all and do not bind.
Let the moment pass,
not through your mind.

When action comes,
you'll know the call.
Not forced, but clear, like
something known.

You are here
to hold the line.
To breathe in Love,
and radiate its sign.

Let Love guide each thought and deed.
A light for others,
in times of need.

◆

Stillness

Stillness,
not silence,
but Source unshaken.
The womb of all motion, never forsaken.

Waves may rise,
and thoughts sway,
but within this stillness,
they lose their way.

Emotions flicker, beliefs decay,
but none can stay where stillness lays.

Let it hold you, just let it cleanse,
no effort made or need to mend.

Here,
Love is not a feeling,
it's a field.
Expansive, whole,
forever healed.

Even one breath
in this space of grace
reforms the world
you thought to face.

So rest awhile, and simply be.
All passes through you,
but you are free.

◇

The Temple Was Never Lost

There was a time we built in stone
what we could not yet hold in flesh.
Temples aligned to Sirius and Sol,
not to worship light,
to receive its rhythm.

Each chamber a resonance field,
and each passage a breath in the body of Earth.
Less monument than tuning forks:
vessels through which memory could descend
and the soul could rise.

We thought the stars lived in the sky.
The ancients knew,
they live within.

The triangle was never just geometry;
it was the collapse of light into form:
Sol, Sirius, Self.
Father, Flame, Mirror.
Outer fire. Inner sun. You.

Those portals still exist,
but not in sand or stone,
in the silence behind your ribs.

Today,
Earth no longer needs monuments
to echo the stars.
She sings them
through you.

The door was never closed.
Only remembrance.
It's not ascension but resonance.

You are not standing before the temple,
but becoming it.

Feel this alignment,
not measured but lived.
Let the chamber open,
not through doors,
but through your breath.

As starlight
meets your heart light,
a flame arises
the ancients could only dream.

What was prismed re-gathered
made clear again
one shining whole.

◆

V.   Refractions of the Real

As perception deepens, reality does not shatter, it refracts.
Truth multiplies, like light through a crystal,
and each angle reveals something new.

This is the alchemy of vision:
where shadow becomes teacher,
and memory, myth, and metaphor
entwine.

Here, the real is not singular but shimmering.
These poems are not conclusions, but lenses,
each one bending light toward a deeper seeing......

"There is a crack in everything,
that's how the light gets in."
— Leonard Cohen

The Principle of Rhythm
"Everything Flows"

The wave pulled back,
not to retreat,
but to return stronger.
I watched the pattern form in stillness.
The code was music.
The music…
was Me.

Tone: G (639 Hz)
Colour: Violet Grey
Resonance: Sacred connection, abstract vision
Alchemical Phase: Rubedo —Reddening, integration, divine union.

Nothing is as it first appears.
Look again. Then again.
Truth arrives refracted
and asks to be seen
sideways.
Even distortion bears a kind of clarity,
when allowed to speak its angle.

◇

Simulation

It's a simulation,
not a metaphor
but a wave-made fact.

Light bends through space,
and space responds back.

What we call life
is layered code,
thought and form,
beliefs bestowed.

Images arise,
then fade to none.
The movie plays,
but the screen is One.

Watch it unfold,
but do not engage.
The drama is loud,
but you are the stage.

Trust in truth,
it doesn't need to prove.
When the Self is known,
illusion moves.

You are eternal, beyond all traits,
not a player,
but that which creates.

◇

Sit

As I sit and reflect,
listening to the non-sense
that appears in my head.

I realize,
it's all out there,
circulating,
dancing with other thoughts
I've been fed.

To feel
these imaginary oscillations
of vibratory sound
without giving it life,

is to open space
for something
beyond strife.

No judgment,
no grasping of wrong or right.

Just balanced awareness,
full of love
and light.

The Point of Awareness

The point of awareness
is where "I Am" lives,
not in thought,
but in what thought gives.

Experience swirls
in radiant dance,
but I remain still,
the infinite glance.

I move with its tides,
rise with its sound,
yet I am the axis
around which it's wound.

The world appears
as something seen,
but it is "I"
who paints the screen.

Not the thinker,
nor the thought,
but the field
in which both are caught.

Be still,
and let it come to you.
All of it returns
when the Seer
is true.

◇

The Philosopher's Flame

Beneath the hush of searching skies,
a question burns that never dies.

Not to gather, not to own,
but to let
what's Real be known.

Through number's gate, the soul begins,
geometry folds the world within.

Form is thought
in sacred spin,
and symmetry reveals the twin.

Sound becomes
the pulse of stars,
music healing ancient scars.

Knowledge bows before its Source.
When ego falters, truth takes course.

The seeker weeps
as veils fall down,
not lost,
but crowned
without a crown.

And in the flame
where names dissolve,
the mirror remains,
and the soul evolves.

◆

Expectation's Alchemy

If I expect,
I grip the thread.
The weave resists,
and the moment fled.

If I meet
this want with grace,
and let the hunger
find its place.

Then, what was tension
melts to breath,
and expectation
meets its death.

No future owed,
no past to keep,
just open hands
in waters deep.

For what I sought
was never gone.
It waits in Now,
where I belong.

◇

Wait-Less

What do we do
while we wait?

Are we surrendering,
or handing life to fate?

The signs are there,
they always glow,
but comfort clings
to the need to know.

You don't need to wait
to see what you'll get.

Be the movement,
not the marionette.

Act not from fear,
but from clear intent,
then what's aligned
will soon be sent.

There is comfort
beyond the fear,
but only after
you've leapt from here.

Waiting can stall
what's already in flight.
So walk your story
and welcome
the light.

◇

Last Breath

I held your hand
as the world fell away.
No time, no fear,
just breath in delay.

Your pulse slowed down,
but your light grew wide,
as if all of Heaven stood just outside.

In that moment,
truth became clear,
from first inhale to final tear.

It's all one breath,
just shaped by form,
the same great fire
through calm and storm.

Your essence now flows
in a different sphere,
but I still feel you,
ever near.

There is no ending,
just shifting planes.
A new beginning
through love's remains.

As in life, so too in death,
you are not gone.
You've just changed breath.

◇

Water-Like

Be like water,
flowing, clear.
No past to hold,
or future to fear.

It doesn't strive,
or cling.
It follows truth
without a string.

You are not
the tides that turn,
nor the waves
that crash and churn.

That's just the surface,
the world outside.
Let the current pass,
you are the tide.

Even if you're just
a drop, it's known.
The ocean lives
in you alone.

So move with grace,
don't resist the fall.
Even when held,
you're not
held at all.

◇

Earth Sound

Can you hear
the Earth beneath,
the silent hum, the subtle wreath?

Not with ears, but with the feet.
A pulsing song, both soft and sweet.

It vibrates in
your steady breath.
A living drum
beneath all death.

Each heartbeat
taps its sacred rhyme.
A dance of stars
through space and time.

You give it life by knowing so,
it lives in you,
above, below.

All it asks
is that you feel.
For feeling is what makes it real.

It is all Love,
the ground, and the flame.

The only constant,

the only name.

◇

Tree Vine

Like a vine
it grew beneath my feet,
with silent threads that softly cheat.

It wound around my waking mind,
binding thought in loops confined.

At first, it seemed a part of me,
just habits, fears, a family tree.

Vines can choke when left unseen.
They strangle hope, and steal the green.

So I traced it back
to the hidden root,
and there I breathed,
and stayed resolute.

No war or fight, just a silent light,
until it softened, and lost its bite.

From that space,
new branches grew.
Seeds of peace,
not just what I knew.

I'll share this fruit
with those in strife.
We all belong
to the Tree of Life.

◇

The Circle You Own

To become aware
of the circle you own
is only the beginning.

The first remembering
that you are
already home.

Once you see
this no-place called life
spinning relative
to your own inner strife,

you'll feel the soul-light
pierce deception's veil,
igniting the heart
where truth prevails.

From that center,
creativity sings.
Intimacy
with everything.

Not through effort,
but harmonic reception.
The Divine cohered
in silent connection.

✳

The Tone Between Worlds

All is sound, yet none can hold it,
not the hand, nor thought that told it.

Vibration hums in stone and star,
in what we were, and what we are.

A bell that tolls at death's soft gate
is a song that dreams reincarnate.

These are not echoes of goodbye,
but chords that fold through earth and sky.

The veil is breath, not wall or bar,
a pause between both near and far.

Music, sung from grief or grace,
can pierce through time, through heart, through place.

For tones remember where we came,
and light responds when called by name.

Beyond the word, beyond the known,
a resonance that feels like home.

Across the veil, they do not speak,
they pulse and shimmer, soft yet deep.

When your heart, in stillness sung,
aligns its beat to what's begun.

You are the bridge, the sound, the door,
and the hum they waited for.

So, sing, not just to hear or play,
but as a light to guide the way.

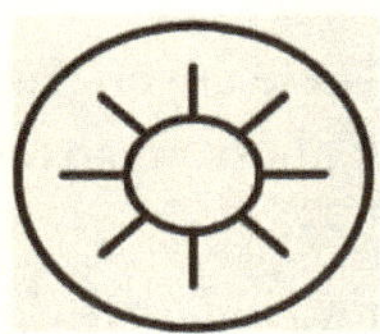

The final light is not the end -
but return

‌✳

VI.   The Light That Remains

What endures beyond unravelling?
Beyond form, fear, seeking?

This final turning is not an end, but a return.
Not to the self as it was,
but to the light that remained all
along.

These are poems of convergence.
They speak not from arrival, but from remembrance.

Here, the light no longer beckons from afar. It burns quietly
at the centre......

"There is light within people of light, and they shine it upon the whole world.
If they do not shine it, what darkness!"
— The Gospel of Thomas, *Logion 24*

The Principle of Cause & Effect and Gender
"Every cause has its effect. Every form bears masculine and feminine"

I no longer chase the source.
I become the Source remembering.
Action and reception.
Thought and birth.
I create as I receive.
And in the
middle…
I dissolve.

Tone: A (963 Hz)
Colour: Radiant White-Gold
Resonance Principle: Unity consciousness / return to Source
Alchemical Phase: Rubedo — Reddening: integration, divine union

What cannot be named, endures.
What cannot be held, remains.
The light you seek is not ahead,
but behind your eyes.

The fading sun brightens within;
beyond twilight,
the dawn.

Stillness

Within the still
where thought has ceased,
the soul inhales
a silent peace.

Emotions rise,
then fall away,
not wrong, not right,
just clouds at play.

This sacred pause,
so vast, so true,
reveals that all
is moving through you.

Stillness is not the absence of waves,
but the sea itself that gently saves.

Here, love abides, not loud, but deep,
a song that sings even when you sleep.

Let it wash, let it mend,
let the silence be your friend.

For in this space,
no lie remains.
Only presence…
Free of chains.

Timeless

There are times
when time dissolves,
when nothing moves,
yet all evolves.

Not forwards or backwards,
just a breath.
Between the birth
and kiss of death.

No clocks to bind,
no roles to play.
Just presence here,
without delay.

The wind may shift,
the light may bend,
but in this stillness,
there's no end.

You cannot chase what always is.
You only need to sit, and witness.

There,
beneath thought's fading chime,
you'll hear the truth:

you were never
in time.

Petal

As a petal falls
to the silent ground,
its space remains,
a sacred sound.

Its colour fades,
its form gives way,
yet nothing true
is lost that day.

The soil receives,
and the light lets go.
A quiet cycle
all beings know.

Decay is not
a final breath,
but transformation
wrapped in death.

Each fall, a bloom
on subtler planes.
Each loss, a whisper
that love remains.

The flower may vanish,
but not the light.
It returns to the bed
from which
it took flight.

Die to Live

Life and death are not apart,
they pulse as one within the heart.

Each breath we take,
each tear we give,
is both a death
and how we live.

Dementia named
what mind forgets,
but soul remembers
without regrets.

You are not
the shell or the face,
but the spark
that holds the space.

To live
is to let go, again.
To walk with loss
and still remain.

Each moment passed is not a theft.
It's just the veil that time has left.

And when you die
to what is gone,
you find you've been
eternal
all along.

The Soft Remains

What stirs inside leaves echoes behind.
A hush in the breath, a bend in the mind.

A sorrow so quiet it forgets to cry,
but lingers still like a closing sigh.

A gentle fear, like twilight rain.
Soft on the skin, deep in the grain.

It doesn't wound, yet it remains:
a whispering thread
through tender veins.

A loving butterfly with trembled wing
wanders through
an uncertain spring.

Its beauty touched
by doubting grace,
yet still it lands,
and still finds its place.

Not every tremble
was meant to still,
or every ache
is an unmet will.

Some things stir to keep us whole.

A soft impression on the soul.

Conductor

With space and distance,
my heart grows whole.
It drinks in love that feeds the soul.

No grasping needed, no false pretense.
Just quiet grace, pure reverence.

In shadow's fold, the light appears,
the self-revealed through silent tears.

And now I know,
I must not smother,
but honour this breath,
this day, this other.

For I am the conductor now,
the vessel through which love learns how
to sing, to move,
to rise, to teach,
to orchestrate
what hearts can't reach.

Together we dance
to love's own beat,
no need for answers,
plans, or speech.

Just moment by moment,
let it unfurl.
The miracle of us,
this bliss-born world.

✳

The Interval of Light

The final sigh is not goodbye,
but the hush
before a new hello.

A breath arriving
from the other side
of knowing.

This is not death,
but the shimmer between forms,
where silence
hums with becoming.

The space between the last and first
is not empty.
It is everything:

The Divine in pause,
the soul in hush,
the heart reweaving
its rhythm with the stars.

Here,
in this breathless blooming,
love waits, light listens,
and life,
unbound by time,
whispers itself
into form again.

But ...What of Truth

Human reason ?
whose whisper we must heed,
so long as we are mind-bound,
speaks of the All,
but cannot part its veil.

Let us not forget:
this unknowing,
this Reality,
this Truth.
Which stands beyond all word,
beyond any form we might name.

Yet,
as human beings,
we move toward our wholeness,
not by grasping Truth,
but by resonating with it.

Not by defining the Absolute,
but by aligning
with what becomes possible
in the shape of our becoming.

It may not be necessary
to declare what Truth is.
For the soul that listens inward,
Truth echoes as this:

We are not apart from it,
not fragments,
but integral to the Whole.

And through love, silence,
resonance and breath,
we may come to remember ourselves
as "it".

Not concept,
lived knowing.
Not belief,
embodied flame,
a flame that remembers
it was always light.

Epilogue: The Third Sun

I did not write this alone.
It arrived like breath....
not summoned by will,
but returned by grace.

The Third Sun came not from thought,
but from stillness:
a warmth behind the ribs
that had always been there,
waiting for me to stop searching outward
long enough to feel it pulse.

I once thought the mirror
was something I carried,
a tool to reflect the world back to itself,
and the flame was something I offered
to light the way for others.

That was only the first turning.
Each spiral since has dissolved
into a deeper veil:
first the illusion of control,
then the identity of the seeker,
then even the need for form.

Now I see:
I am not the mirror; I am not the flame.

I am the light they both point to:
the third presence.
Neither seen, nor touched, but known
when nothing else remains.

The Third Sun is not new.
It is ancient memory, rising again in this now.
Not a sun in the sky,
but a radiance within the soul's architecture,
burning to clarify.

It does not rise.
It returns.

With its return,
I remember:
I was never writing these words
to reveal anything,
only to peel away what was not.

There are no more teachings.
Only this:

The fire was never mine.
The light was never apart.
The sun never left.

Now,
I no longer seek
to hold the mirror
or carry the flame.

I stand within them both,
as they pass through me as light returning to light.

This is the Third Sun.
It does not end the spiral.

It reveals it was always **whole.**

About the Author

John Den-Kaat walks the spiral path
where poetry, spirit, and art converge.
After decades in the healing arts, he
tended to the body, yet it was the soul's
quiet whisper that drew him deeper into
the realms where memory stirs and truth
burns softly.

His words arise from remembering rather
than instructing. They are both mirrors
and flames: reflecting the light that
endures through every darkness, and the
darkness that gives shape to every light.

His work moves between pen, brush,
dance, and road, each a way of listening to
the harmony threaded through all things.

These journeys, inward and across the world, have carried him toward
threshold spaces between grief and grace, departure and return, silence and
sound.

From such crossings his poems emerge, where maps dissolve into the
liminal terrain of meditation, travel, solitude, and the slow unfolding of
inner alchemy.

A Mirror for the Flame follows his first book, *See the Dark; Feel the Light*,
extending his offering of words as prayer and as invitation into the spiral of
becoming.

Born in Scotland and now living in Australia, he inhabits horizons wide
enough to hold both his silence and his song.

Acknowledgements

To those who listened
when I needed silence.

To those who held space
while I found my shape.

To those whose wisdom, presence,
or quiet encouragement
helped this book come into being,
you know who you are.

Each spark, insight and
thread offered along the way
has been woven into these pages.

This book is not mine alone,
it is the reflection of many mirrors,

lit by a shared flame.

Reflections with the Flame

This book is a living mirror,
shaped through rhythm, silence, and breath.

It moves as a spiral —
inward, outward, and inward again.
Each poem was born from stillness.
Each reflection opens like a petal.
Each turning carries a tone of becoming.

The Light That Remains is not reached,
but revealed
when striving quiets.

You are here for a reason.
Something in you recognised these words.
Let them speak where they need to,
and rest where they do not.

You may return to these pages
and discover them changed,
because you will have changed.
This is the nature of spirals.
This is how remembering works.

Simply being present
is already enough.

There comes a moment
when all movement gathers,
when going inward and outward
feel like the same breath.

This is the Terium Quid:
the stillness at the heart of motion.
Not emptiness,
but quiet fullness
before things divide.

Here, light remembers its source,
and life gently draws itself home.

Every spiral has a centre.
As energy gathers,
opposites meet and soften.
This is not about leaving our humanity,
but holding it fully,
light and shadow, strength and tenderness,
in one coherent field.

The spiral remembers through stillness.

"There is a still point of the turning world.
Neither flesh nor fleshless;
neither from nor towards;
at the still point, there the dance is."
— T.S. Eliot, *Four Quartets*

In that still point,
the pause between creating and letting go,
we awaken as beings of light,
not leaving the world,
but loving it more deeply.

Here, flame and mirror become one.
The Third Sun rises:
a quiet knowing,
a gentle love.

This is your invitation.

Whatever rises within you
does not need fixing or forcing.
When life loosens its grip,
allow your hand to open.
When life asks for your presence,
offer it freely.

Both moments are sacred.

As you move through each turning,
whether dissolving or becoming,
remember that you walk as flame
within the spiral of life.

So, walk gently now.
Your presence matters.

Thank you
for meeting yourself here.

The next breath is yours ......

Field of Petals

A Holy Rain

Sit

Circus

Space

Conductor

Stillness

Cornered

Stranger's Smile

Creepy Friend

Temporary

Groove

Dad

The Alchemy of Expectation

Die to Live

The Circle You Own

Dive Deep

The Eerie Pause

Down

The Interval of Light

Duo

The Philosopher's Flame

Earth Sound

❧ The Point of Awareness

❧ First Rehearsal   ❧ The Soft Remains

                  ❧ Hamster Wheel   ❧ Theatrical Illusion

        ❧ Last Breath   ❧
Timeless

❧ Non-sense   ❧ Traditional

                  ❧ Petal   ❧ Tree
Vine

        ❧ Precious Life   ❧ Wait-Less

            ❧ Rip   ❧ Walk the Path; "Art"

                  ❧ Shadows in Awareness
❧ Water-Like

    ❧ Shell Release   ❧ Where the Heart and Mind
Meet

              ❧ Simulation   ❧ Yes

FIELD NOTES

A Lexicon of Harmonic Echoes
(Not definitions, but doors.)

◐ **THE MIRROR** Reflection that does not lie, revealing the self in its many veils and unveilings.

✳ **THE FLAME** Illumination and transformation, the fire that clarifies without consuming.

◉ **THE BREATH** The first gesture of awareness, the last note of return. Inhale as becoming; exhale as release. The book's pulse lives here.

〜 **THE ECHO** Not sound but return. The curved breath of your own being, folded back through memory. Resonating remembrance, without words.

••• **THE VEIL** The thin place between seen and unseen, a breath-like threshold entered through presence.

∘ **THE FIELD** The silent ground of emergence. Neither page nor author, but the listening presence in which words take root.

◯ **THE SEED** The hidden beginning, silent potential, what listens before it breaks open.

❧ **THE PETAL** Each poem is a petal: distinct, fragile, whole, yet part of a greater bloom. The spiral is their stem.

♀ **LILITH** The frequency withheld. Not a narrative but tone. The third note unsounded. When held, she becomes coherence.

⌂ **TEMPLE** Not stone, but resonance; the chamber within where light and breath converge.

⬘ **TERIUM QUID** The centre of the spiral. The heart of balanced interchange. The still point between opposites and the third field that holds light and shadow, masculine and feminine, in coherent balance. Not a thing, but the field of awareness through which all things meet.

⛾ **THE WITHHELD WAVEFORM** What you once exiled in order to survive. Now returning, not to disrupt you, but to complete the chord.

☉ **THE THIRD SUN** An inner radiance, not in the sky, but within. Clarifying rather than consuming. It does not rise; it returns.

🌀 **THE SPIRAL** The geometry of becoming, ever returning and revisiting truth from wider octaves of awareness. A path of remembrance.

✳ **FREQUENCY CODES** Each stage holds a living tone. These are not fixed assignments but resonant fields. Sonic invitations that mirror what is already heard.

◇ **HARMONIC RESONANCE** The felt coherence when body, symbol, word, and soul begin to sing the same note.

↺ **RESONANT TURNINGS** Six movements of the spiral. These are not chapters but tonal thresholds, each bearing colour, frequency, and an inner alchemy.

♏ **ALCHEMICAL RESONANCE** Nigredo, Albedo, Citrinitas, Rubedo. The four phases of becoming. The invisible unfolding of inner change expressed through form.

✦ **MAGNUM OPUS** The Great Work of transformation: the soul's unfolding from darkness into gold, a remembering that reveals what has already been present.

Harmonic Notes on the Frequencies

These tones are the doorways of remembrance.

Each frequency is a key. An opening chamber within body, heart, and soul. Listen not only with the ear, but with your very being.

The mappings here: of tone, colour, and resonance, were chosen intuitively.

They are not prescriptions, but reflections: mirrors of traditions that have long carried the understanding that sound is not just heard but lived.

Sources of inspiration include:

- The Solfeggio Frequencies: ancient tonal scales held in sacred sound traditions and modern vibrational healing.
- Archetypal colour resonance: colours long associated with chakric, elemental, and metaphysical fields.
- The Magnum Opus of Alchemy: the stages of transformation, echoed here as tonal thresholds of refinement.
- The Hermetic Principles (The Kybalion): particularly the principle of vibration, that all is movement, all is sound.

Structured as a spiral of harmonic frequencies and alchemical imagery, this book does not present stages of awakening, but lenses of attention, inviting the reader toward remembrance rather than ascent.